I0617281

Tiny Little Landslides

Micro Essays

Grace Evanoff

Wet Cement Press

Berkeley, Asheville, Reno

Tiny Little Landslides ©2025
by Grace Evanoff

ISBN 979-8-9918692-0-1

Library of Congress Control Number: 2025933074

The Sideways Tree edition

Cover art by Jen Carmiel

Acknowledgments: I'd like to thank Wet Cement Press and, specifically, my editor, Thoreau Lovell, for seeing *Tiny Little Landslides* through with me.

Wet Cement Press
1908 Yolo Ave
Berkeley, CA 94707

*I dedicate this book to my loving & wonderful
husband, Matthew Evanoff*

Contents

Tiny Little Landslides

ON BREVITY

Women are keen on brevity because, for centuries, we've been cutting our words short, slipping one-liners out the sides of our mouths to our friends, and getting our point across as fast as we can before we're interrupted or told to stop.

On the Untold Story of the Sick American Woman

I know a woman who set her life on fire. I know two actually. No, three. Three women who set their lives on fire because—no four, I know four women who set—no five, sorry, no six! I know six women who set their lives on fire because they couldn't do it anymore. In a Nelson Algren, "I just can't" kind of way, in a Shakespearean, operatic "O" appraisal, a nod to every Girl Interrupted.

Everyone always knew what was right for them. They needed this, they needed that. "If only they listened." They shut them up, diagnosed them into apathy, and called them, "sick." And their cure? More nothing.

But what if.

What if they needed culture? A history to hold onto. Lovers. They should have left. They should have run. They'd still be themselves if they'd had fresh flowers and sleep and poetry. They needed a reinvention of their senses. They needed another language other than English to express the freedom of their loneliness and the poisonous well of our Western hope. But they couldn't, and in the face of another groundhog day—man, they just did what they could.

On Explaining Art

I say it best when I say it like this, anything I say after this, even about this piece in particular, will be a
limited translation of what I originally meant when I
wrote it. Every question about inspiration, and what
made me think of writing this piece will only be some
of the truth, because this is the best translation of the
creativity, and just because you can deconstruct art
doesn't mean you can make it whole again, or at all.

ON THE ORIGIN STORY

I'm in middle school rehearsing a play. My director wants more from me. "Come on," he says. "You're the biggest drama queen I know." For the next three days, I think about our impending confrontation.

I write a letter inquiring as to the whereabouts of his formal theater training and question whether he could feel the precise moment all my respect came crashing down like violent hail in the cruelest winter storm. The only reason I don't deliver that letter is because I cannot reconcile how dramatic it would be. Instead, I begin my lifelong journey with silent resentment.

On Astrid's Garden

Astrid will be eighty next year. She lives a full life and has been everywhere and met everyone. In her studio, not even front and center, is a picture of her with her late husband and President Obama. She has a big backyard full of luscious plants and treasures from her travels as a photographer. The rest of the treasures are from thrift stores or gifts from people who want to be a part of her magic. One of the backyard's main attractions is a tree that's grown sideways. Everyone loves this tree, because it's special. I've been in her backyard more than a handful of times, and each time I'm there, someone will say to me, "Have you seen this tree?" "I have," I tell them. "I love it." They love it too, which is why they wanted to share it with me to begin with. I'm sure she was advised to cut it down at some point, but instead she let it be. People sit on it, awe at it, take pictures with it, and treat it like it's the best tree in the backyard. Meanwhile, there are other trees that are just as big and sprouting with the greenest leaves, but they don't grow sideways, they're just regular trees that shoot straight up like rockets towards the sky. The sideways tree is such a hit because people can't believe that it didn't break. The tree was meant to be in Astrid's backyard, because only someone as creative and kind as Astrid could have the intelligence to leave something so unique alone long enough for it to grow into something beautiful.

ON TALENT

The best actress in Los Angeles doesn't act anymore. Born and raised in Los Angeles, she looks like a movie star and has that special spark no amount of money or training could produce. I've watched people trip over themselves trying to get a second look. Of course, nobody knows her as the best actress in Hollywood. When she's not in and out of mental institutions, or jail, she works odd jobs and drinks herself into oblivion. She can do it all: Tennessee Williams, Chekhov, Shakespeare, anything. It's not for lack of ego either, she's aware of her gift, burdened by it. The reason you don't know her is because she's tortured, and only nice when she drinks. When she doesn't drink, she's cruel and tries to break up friend groups for sport so everyone can be as lonely as she is.

On Colleen

There was a woman in Chicago who was known as "queen" of the theater scene. She was a decent actor, always front and center in the hottest new show, and since we just so happened to have a mutual friend in common, we'd often run into each other at parties and events. Then I moved in with that mutual friend, so we saw each other even more. No matter the occasion, no matter the setting, no matter the time, no matter how sober or intoxicated she was, she would introduce herself to me as if we'd never met. At first, I thought she was just stupid, so I played along when it happened the first ten times.

Our conversations were never deep since we never got past introductions. Then one night, it dawned on me, that this was a purposeful power tactic. No one gave me that intel. It was something I gleaned from the duper's delight that spread across her face as I introduced myself for the sixteenth time that year. If we had been auditioning for the same roles, or going after the same lovers, I might have understood such a show of energy, but the efforts were wasted on a little nobody like me. Surely, as the queen of the theatre scene, she must have had real competition. There must have been ladies in waiting just foaming at the mouth for her fall from grace.

Why she chose to play such a game with a peasant like myself actually brought me nothing but pure joy. I began looking forward to her arrival at parties, asking everyone if she was coming, so we could play our game. I even started initiating it by introducing myself the moment she walked in the door. The first time I did it, I could see the queen's gears working overtime. Undefeated in her pettiness, and psychotically committed to her role, she decided to play along, and for the seventeenth time that year, we made our first introductions.

On Journals

My parents sent me all my old journals.

My personal journals are filled to the brim, pages swollen from ink, but the journals I was required to keep for school are barely touched. Where the personal journals are all too forthcoming, the assigned journals might leave a reader wanting.

I see this trend begin in my assigned journal from second grade. In one entry, I write, "I have a lot of secrets." My teacher writes back, "What kind of secrets? You can always share with me!"

Too comfortable for my liking, I ice her out and go back to rote entries, like, "My name is Grace, and I like writing in journals."

On Friendship

My friend Johnny from Chicago is visiting me in Los Angeles. It's only been a few months, but I've missed him.

LATER:

I got Johnny too high tonight, and now he's freaking out because I live next door to the Scientology building. He's convinced himself that I'm a Scientologist, and that the only reason I invited him over is to recruit him into Scientology. I tried to convince him otherwise, but he fell asleep watching me.

ON A CERTAIN SMALL AIRPORT IN LA COUNTY

Once in a great while, I fly out of a certain airport in Los Angeles County. On rare occasions, this airport boards two different flights at the same time. On two different airplanes. As a civilian, I understand this might be an overwhelming task. But as an alleged airport, one would think two flights boarding at the same time would be manageable. One would expect a little preparation from an airport.

See, in the past, if you were, say, I don't know, in a hurry, and pushed in a million directions by airport staff, you may have made the mistake of getting on the WRONG PLANE. How can that possibly be true, you might wonder. You might say, "I thought getting on the wrong plane was something that only happens in the movies." I was naive like that once.

Then one day you'll be sitting on an airplane, and the pilot will announce the details of your Seattle destination, when you're actually supposed to be heading to Sacramento. If you're really lucky, you'll get to watch the plane you were scheduled to be on—take off. Just. like. the. movies. You'll even get to scream "STOP THE PLANE," and they actually will.

ON THE BOOKSTORE

I got hired because of my proximity to the bookstore. My folks lived within walking distance, and since I was living with them due to an early life crisis, it worked out perfectly. I could get to the bookstore in ten minutes if someone flaked. In my first week, I mentioned that I was a morning person, and became the "opener" immediately. Within a month I was opening the store at 5:30AM six days a week and getting off around two or three. It was a dream job. Being the sole opener fell into perfect sync with my depression schedule. No one batted at an eye when I turned in at 7PM, like I was twenty-four going on ninety.

"I have to open in the morning," I would say to my friends, to my parents, to the Internet, "So I'm going to bed."

Then with the sun still ablaze shining through my sister's old bedroom's window, I would smoke a bowl of marijuana, turn on Netflix, and nap for fourteen hours until society needed me again. I would dream of my job because that's the only thing I had room for in my subconscious, besides all the fear and terror that led me there to begin with.

I learned the computer system in fifty-five seconds because there was just one working computer and it was a beige Macintosh from the late eighties. Then I learned how to cut strips off the top of the New York Times and every other newspaper we carried to prove to the vendor that we weren't cutting them short and saying we sold fifteen newspapers instead of sixteen newspapers. It was busy work, and I was happy to do something with absolutely no meaning or consequence, it was a fucking relief.

Since the elders and I were on the same schedule, they'd sometimes beat me to my 5:30AM opening and get into the pile of newspapers, leaving the exact amount they owed. Except the tax. Never the tax. There was this one woman with great red hair and even cuter overalls who scoffed every single time I rang her up. Like, I'm so sorry California tax laws haven't been reinvented since you were here two days ago. Why is that my responsibility? Instead of reaching in her own pockets, she'd scrape change from the little blue "leave a penny, take a penny" cup, also from the late 80's. One time, when she was feeling particularly enraged with California tax laws, she looked me dead in the eye and said, "You happy?" I was never happy, but her misplaced rage made me feel good in comparison, so I said, "Yes, thank you so much," and she never spoke to me again.

On Van Gogh

When I went to Amsterdam, I visited the Van Gogh museum. It bothered me how everyone took photos of the paintings instead of actually looking at the paintings. Why not save yourself the trip and the money, and just use Google?

I find a comfort in my disdain for others, but as I'm learning in my weekly trauma-informed therapy sessions, this particular comfort does not equate to health.

In fact, because of these weekly trauma-informed therapy sessions I now ask myself, why are you triggered? Oh, you hate this? Interesting. What is it about this thing you supposedly hate that you actually hate in yourself?

Because taking a picture of something beautiful is actually pretty innocent, isn't it? Taking a picture of something beautiful, so you can prove you were a part of it seems human. And aren't you always kvetching about the lack of humanity? And maybe I'm not taking pictures of Van Gogh, but how many times have I tried and failed to capture a beautiful sunset, only to go online and see everyone else has done the same? One time, after I posted a Chicago sunset my mother-in-law asked "What am I supposed to be looking at?"

I was disappointed to realize my amateur photography on an iPhone didn't capture the way light bounced, or the many shades of pink present, but at least I tried. And that's what most people are doing, right? Just trying.

On What Stuck

After I visited Anne Frank's house I couldn't stop thinking about one part of the story I had never really thought about before: Anne Frank's, father, Otto Frank and his hope. Up until the moment the family was betrayed by one of their closest friends, Otto Frank was making markings on a map using hat pins to keep track of the progress made by allies. They were getting closer and closer to Amsterdam...and then someone close to the family gave them up, and the rest is a horrible history. Yet, Otto survived it all. Is that a blessing or a curse?

ON A REAL MASTER'S ANSWER

A real master of the craft is not arrogant to newcomers. They do not scoff at the beginner's questions, they welcome them. I once was in a Q & A with a famous actress, a master of her craft, and I asked a question that we had been told as beginners never to ask. Or maybe I learned to stop asking because I had seen my peers shot down one time too many. To ask about the process was to admit we didn't have our own yet. What hubris to rob a beginner from being a beginner because you don't have the clarity of thought to answer a question. When I did ask my question, which was "Is there anything you look for in scripts when you're developing your character?" Like clockwork, there were scoffs. But the master looked at me for a second, and said, "Yes, I look for opposites. What they say versus what they do. What other people say about them versus what they think of themselves."

ON STEINBECK

I wonder what Steinbeck would think of his museum in Salinas. I don't think he'd like it. However, I do think he'd come to the grand opening and be polite about it. I think he'd shake hands and even pose for a picture or two, kindly decline any spirits offered to him, because he quit drinking in 1988, maybe he'd even sign another first edition. I think people would expect him to stay for a couple hours so he could regale them with his stories but after about forty minutes he'd grow tired of the pretenses and end up shooting the shit outside with one of the caterers.

The influential elite of Salinas hated Steinbeck while he was alive, but once they realized his name is what would keep them relevant for centuries to come, they worship him. Is that history in their museum?

On the Saddest Things

It was 3AM and the beginning of a Chicago winter. A man in nice cowboy boots asked me why I got into theater. I was in my early twenties and over everything. "I guess it feels like the only place I can be myself," I said. The man in nice cowboy boots snorted a line of coke off an old picture of a friend that had recently passed away, and said, "That's the saddest thing I ever heard."

On Getting Help

There are many retreats for this type of crisis, and even more well-meaning videos and recycled quotes. They call it the dark night of the soul, trials and tribulations, major depressive disorder. I call it the year without hope or the year without music or the year of stasis. They say people like me have to learn to let things go, but that's hard for a person whose natural instinct is to hold on. For the person who never forgets. When you're in this story, it feels like there's no number to call, there's no group to go to, and there's no tea to drink. When you're in this story, you have to wade through time like the ocean in a storm.

On Neighbors

When I grabbed two doggy bags instead of one, I heard one of my neighbors tell another neighbor, "I hate when people do that."

What does she hate? I thought two bags at a time was kosher.

Her words run though my head for days, it's all I can hear, as I open a cupboard, as I take out the trash, as I eat my dinner. It's like a demented Thomas the Train, I hate when people do that, I hate when people do that, I hate when people do that.

On Tiny Little Landslides

These tiny little landslides keep me awake, like the dead man's heart. The kind of emotions that get you through the side and go straight through the gut. The therapist says we'll meet on Tuesdays and "let's meet on Thursdays too…and actually, I need you to fill out this sheet of paper in case you decide to do something irreversible and we can't get ahold of you."

"And here's a chart to track these emotions, sorry, these tiny little landslides. See if we can pinpoint where the mind and body start to weather, and then what happens? And where do you feel it? It's important to become mindful if you want to control the damage."

"And here's a guided meditation really, a mantra, okay, it's a script for self-compassion because you are lacking. As in you have zero, nil, negative actually, I mean you hate yourself, and it's showing, it's overpowering and paralytic."

I walk with the script, repeat the words until I mean it, until I can feel it, in my mind, and in my body, and the script works. I used to be an actress after all, I commit to the role of someone who loves themselves, who has enough fortitude to fight these emotions, these tiny little landslides, off.

On Being a Cohen or a Dylan

I wish I could be more like Leonard Cohen, but I'm more like Dylan. I think of Leonard Cohen the Buddhist, the spiritual man, the man who knew how to rise above it all and write about matters of the heart. Meanwhile, Dylan is in the mud, he's in the thick of it, he's in reality and he can't escape it, he can't unsee it, he can't go to the top of the mountain and meditate his way out of it. He has to take the long way, the hard way. He has to dig himself out of his own grave, throw his own wake. Dylan can't accept things as they are, he has to fight them as they come. How nice it must be to be a Cohen.

ON OPTOMETRISTS

When I was little I wanted glasses. I actually wanted an identity, but thought the glasses might help. Even then I knew a good costume could go a long way, and thought glasses might inspire some respect.

Everyone knew my vision was perfect, but I insisted I couldn't see the chalkboard. Really, I was just bad at math, and everyone knew that too.

When I got to the optometrist, my mom had a private word with her, and then the optometrist sat me down alone, placed the machinery in front of my eyes, and made a bunch of clicks and whooshes with a variety of lenses.

I did the whole act, I had my lines down pat. At the beginning, I acted like I couldn't see anything. That was a lie though. Not only could I see the letters, I could count the tiny molecules of dust on said letters.

After a few more minutes of theatrics, the optometrist plastered on the smuggest smile in the world, and stuck her pencil into the empty lenses to reveal there was nothing actually there to begin with. I had been looking through empty holes the entire time. A true "gotcha" moment.

"You don't need glasses," she said. I blacked out from embarrassment, and don't remember anything that followed, but years later when I failed my driving test because I couldn't see, I felt a sense of relief that my time had finally come.

On Sitting at the Café

I sat at the café and watched a dad push his baby girl in the stroller up and down the block while she slept. Up and down, up and down, up and down, up and down. He stopped once, and she woke up, burst into tears, and threw her blanket off. The power struggle began. Dad wanted to keep it on, and the little baby girl never wanted to ever see the blanket again. She won, and the dad went back to pushing her stroller. Then she snuggled up into a little cocoon, the sun as her blanket now, and fell back asleep with a mischievous smile.

ON BOUNDARIES

When my mom is done texting me, even if we're in the middle of a conversation, she just writes "xo." When my husband is dozing off at night, and I'm still telling him a story, he kisses the air in front of him to let me know he's done listening. When I want to stop talking to someone, I just keep listening and suffer.

ON SCARING THE SCAMMER

After one hundred and something job applications, I finally got scammed. It was bound to happen sooner or later. I'd like to think I was too clever to get scammed, but the desperation combined with my brain size decreasing six percent due to pregnancy finally got to me. I knew something was wrong when they asked for my driver's license, but I decided to not listen to my instincts, and give them access to my most personal information anyway. My brain finally woke up when they sent me a text asking for my social security number. And perhaps it's the desperation and my brain size decreasing six percent due to pregnancy, but after I reported my license as stolen, ordered a new one, and froze my credit, a surge of vengeance coursed through my body. I may be a year into trauma-informed therapy, and about to be a new mother, but I am still me.

I decided that instead of acting scared and begging them not to use my information, I would tell them to go ahead and do what they want. After all, since they now had my San Diego address, I welcomed them to come and visit, but to make sure they knew I was surrounded by military personnel and a plethora of second-amendment Karen's who watched the neighborhood waiting for their chance to become a hero. For the first time since the scamming begun, there was silence. Maybe they weren't scared, but at the very least, they thought, "Wow, this bitch is psychotic." I felt my life force rushing back, so I decided to send them another text, just to seal the deal. "I'm so glad we met," I wrote, signing off with a little smiley face.

ON LUCY

It's the summer before we graduate from Cal State Fullerton with theater degrees. Lucy's going through a major spiritual transformation, she's just found God, and driving to Northern California to visit me. "Grace," she says on the voicemail. "See you soon. Everything is amazing." I didn't think she would drive eight hours on a whim. I thought it was just something someone says when they mix marijuana and cocaine.

Hours later, there she is, knocking on my door wearing nothing but a rainbow poncho and Hello Kitty flip-flops. She hugs me hard and whispers in my ear, "I grew up this summer. I'm ready to be a good friend to you now."

Then we take a walk through town, and she throws herself at a tree.

"Look how it sparkles," she says.

"That's a fake tree, Lucy."

"Listen to it sing." She closes her eyes and leans up against it, with one leg straddled on each side.

"The tree is not real."

"Shhhh, just listen."

The next day, we drive back to Orange County in separate cars, and Lucy agrees to pick up toiletries for our apartment. She makes it to Target but forgets everything on the list. Instead, she opens the door to our apartment donning new costume butterfly wings and matching fake orange lashes.

Already understanding that the mission went awry, I ask, "Did you at least get toilet paper?"

Lucy rolls her eyes, and let's out an audible sigh. "I'll be back," she says, turning around, gripping the edge of her right butterfly wing so it doesn't get caught in the door.

ON BOURDAIN IN LA

Anthony Bourdain swore he could never live here. He found the LA sun oppressive. There's a lot of pressure to be happy in this climate, and when you're grieving in ninety-degree weather, it feels like the sun is mocking you.

On Robin

The last time I saw him, he bought the latest Wired magazine and the new Salinger biography. We exchanged niceties and he recognized me from all the other times I didn't bother him.

The day he passed, my coworkers and I displayed a small photo of him by the register. When the owner popped by, she took one look at our memorial and said, "This is ugly, he looks sad." She left and came back with a whole new picture. "A happier one." Then she pulled out two miniature LED candles from her purse, framed his face, and let out a sigh of relief. "Much better," she said.

I see what Robin Williams was talking about all those years. Some people just make you feel alone.

On Witches

I met three witches this past week.

One worked at the makeup store Ulta, the second one was interviewing me for a job teaching kids how to read, and I met the third one while sipping a strawberry-vanilla soda outside of a Middle Eastern market in Normal Heights.

The Ulta witch was a grandma with the skin of an un-traumatized twenty-year-old. As she applied my foundation, she talked about her grandchild, and then started in on me: She said she could tell I don't take care of myself enough, that I go until I drop, and she could feel it in her knees. She correctly surmised that my husband was a gentle soul, whereas I was "a feisty one."

The second witch who was interviewing me for a job broke every employment law protecting pregnant women that's ever existed. As soon as I walked in she asked when I was due, and when I said, "November," she took a better look and said, "That's right." Then she asked my horoscope and my husband's horoscope, and the baby's horoscope. Me and the baby are Scorpios, so we didn't get that job.

The third witch, in her 80's, the eldest of them, walked by me, stopped, took a few steps back, pointed at my stomach, and said, "BOY!"

"That's right," I told her. Both of her caretakers looked at each other, impressed. "Wow," they said. And before she got on her way, she said, "But he will look like you!"

On Womanhood

Today a sweet puppy came and said hello to me in the bar. She immediately got her first period. I had to tell her owner. "Um, there's—there's blood—she's bleeding, but she's fine." The poor man looked so concerned, "Oh no! What happened!?" Oh God, I thought, I'm not prepared for this. I didn't leave the safe confines of my apartment today, thinking I would have to explain the process of a menstrual cycle to a stranger. And lucky for me, I didn't have to. The second I said it was her period, he looked at me like I'd pulled out a weapon and abandoned the establishment, leaving the small pool of blood behind him for someone else to clean up.

On Groveling

It's the first year of my Masters' Program. There's drama going on with a certain student production. According to office gossip, one of the grad students, Joey, made a comment about his "stupid prop" in front of the entire cast and crew.

That's all the information I have. I don't know the exact stupid prop Joey is allegedly referring to. However, I do know that this kind of conduct is considered blasphemy in the theater. A prop person could give you a scarf slathered in human feces, and you better act like it's hot off the runway.

Joey now has to be publicly humiliated and shamed so he can grow from this process and never do anything wrong again. His apology tour is on its second day. He's stopping by each office, standing up in each class, whispering to people in corners. Disgraced politicians do less apologizing than this. Then again, at least they understand that a thousand apologies will never be enough when people like to watch you grovel.

On Galina

It's 2009 and Galina is teaching us the Stanislavsky Acting System. Stanislavsky has a saying, "Leave your coat at the door." Meaning leave all your personal nonsense behind before you enter the room. Now, I literally leave my coat outside the door because I fear I'll never come out, and I want people to know I'm missing. I'm not sure what Galina will do with me exactly if I die from fear in her class; Maybe she'll use me as a prop.

Galina is not one to mince words, and for some reason, we pay no mind to her name-calling and the utter annihilation of our "weak little egos." But one day, she admonishes America in one of her rants, and as a class, we decide that's our final straw. We're too afraid to revolt against Galina's Anti-Americanism to her face, so we do it behind her back instead.

We agree to hide a teeny-tiny American flag on the stage, in every single scene, for the rest of the semester. It was Chekhov who said nothing unites people like a common enemy, and he was right. As a class, we've never been more united. Now that we have a flag to hide we all "help" each other set up our scenes. In reality, we are blocking Galina's view.

At first, we put the American flag in places completely unseen to the naked eye, but we were comforted by its mere existence. However, as weeks pass, and in traditional American fashion, we become brazen. We start allowing the flag to peek out of its confined territory. By the end of the semester, we're working on a piece from A Doll's House, and the American flag is sticking out of a vase, practically in full view. Galina walks in and takes in our set. For a moment we think our cover is blown, but alas, she's just admiring our dedication to set design. "I love that bouquet of flowers you guys!"

"You do?" I asked. Half of us in a fit of giggles. "Yes," she said. "A lot." Then she went back to cleaning her nails.

My classmate Billy got smart and almost blew our gig. "We love it too actually, you could even say we pledge our allegiance to it." Thank God she ignores us.

On Social Media

During the rehearsal of a play, one of the stagehands tagged me and all my classmates as celebrities he thinks we look like. He tagged me as Glen Close playing Cruella de Ville, Lucille Ball, and Paris Hilton. I'm grateful that he understands my range as a person, but also feel a little exposed.

On Being a Cactus

My friend told me years ago that I'm a cactus. I'm the kind of friend that doesn't need a lot of water. You don't need to tend to me often, and I'll still be there, standing strong, full, and ready to offer water if anyone else needs some. It was meant as a compliment because they saw themselves as a cactus, too. And at that time, it was exactly how I wanted to be seen: A creature who didn't need other people to survive.

I don't think I'm a cactus anymore. Maybe it was COVID, maybe it was the breakdown, maybe it was the breakthrough, maybe it was pregnancy, maybe it was birth, maybe it was motherhood, or maybe I've never been a cactus.

I need people more than I'd like to admit. I need community. I need people to agree with, to argue with, to mourn with, to celebrate with, to be bored with, to be excited with, to eat with, to drink with, to do nothing with, to do everything with, to pick out a cactus with. I think I'm supposed to feel some kind of shame in this admittance.

But at the risk of sounding as dramatic as I am, wouldn't the real shame be in these missed experiences because I was too prideful and hurt to admit that I—a human—not a cactus—god forbid, need other humans.

ON WILD-CARDS

My in-laws live in a quaint part of San Diego. Everyone is mild-mannered for the most part, but there are some wild-cards, and in a neighborhood like this, the wild-cards can't hide. For example, at the food truck the other night, one of the wild-cards had a few bottles of wine under her belt and lost her shoe. She hobbled around for at least thirty minutes with just one pink flat on her right foot. When I pointed out the lost shoe, which was right under our noses the entire time, she shrugged and said she didn't feel like putting it back on. I decided right then I liked her a lot.

ON TEENAGERS

I was sitting with my four-month-old outside of a pizza place in San Diego when a teenager walked by, took out a multi-colored vape, and blew the perfect cloud of smoke into my baby's face. I pulled the cover over his stroller and said, "Are you out of your mind!?" If I take my baby to a bar or a strip club, sure, I should expect some smoke to be blown in his face, maybe even a thimble of coke to be slipped into his onesie. The teenager turned around, shocked to see a baby being enveloped by his cloud of bubble-gum-scent cancer, and literally gasped. "I'm so sorry," he said, taking the wind right out of my furious sails. "Oh," I said. "Thanks. Okay." And off he went, un-bothered and unburdened by a fully formed frontal cortex. I want better for this teenager. His response made me like him. I thought: there's hope for this kid, he's cool, he should be smoking real cigarettes.

ON THE WISE MAN

There is a wise man I listen to, or rather "follow," but social media has taken him over. He insists on saying one wise thing every day so his algorithm doesn't falter because if his algorithm falters, then he can't make a living, and if he can't make a living being wise, then he's going to be destitute, and if he's destitute, he'll still be wise, but no one will hear his wisdom, and since these are the technological cards he was dealt, he has to play this technological hand, but he is stretching this gift thin. Even the wisest man cannot be wise every day. He goes from Confucius to Snapple Cap about four times a week now. It would be a lot more valuable if he were just Confucius three times a week, but the algorithm only cares about its value, not his, not mine, not yours, not ours.

ON THANKSGIVING

There's a bartender in Ocean Beach that everyone calls, "Bangs." I went to her bar on Thanksgiving, and she wouldn't let a group of European tourists come in because they had a baby with them. A sympathetic patron turned around to try and help, "Unless the baby's twenty-one?" Unfortunately, for everyone, the baby was not twenty-one. The Europeans looked even more offended, and I sympathized with them. I don't think they wanted to get the baby drunk, and even if they did, is that really our business?

After they left, Bangs was outraged. "I mean it's a baby! In a bar! Who brings their baby to a bar!?" I wanted to raise my hand and say, "Well, actually, Bangs, I was practically raised in an Irish pub, and I'm still standing," but I could tell she was an emotional person to begin with, and I didn't want to start a fight with someone so outraged about a baby, especially on Thanksgiving, the national holiday of fighting. Bangs was fighting her own battle and I didn't need to add to her stress, but when she started to cry as the national anthem played for the afternoon football game, I had to pay my bill and leave. It was all too much. There's no such a thing as a safe place on Thanksgiving.

On Kindness

Nobody has kinder in-laws than I do. They harass me with their kindness. Every day is another nightmare of them going out of their way to make my life easier. I go to sleep with their words replaying in my head. Is there anything you need? I made your favorite meal. We got the white wine you like!

When our ceiling caves in and we have to hunker down at their place, they do nothing but make accommodations. One day, my mother-in-law comes into our room four times in the span of forty minutes to see if she can hold the baby while I take a shower, if she's cooking something for dinner I will enjoy, if there's any laundry that needs to be done, and just to tell me what a good mother I am. What fresh hell is this?

When my husband has to leave for night classes on Tuesday, and I isolate myself to an office in the back of the house, she goes across the street to drink wine with the neighbors. While there, she texts me three times to make sure I'm okay with exclamation marks that imply I might not be, which is...fair. Once in a while I give in to these gestures, but only because it would be rude not to, and my therapist says I need to accept help where it's offered. Fine then. I suppose an extra blanket wouldn't hurt, yes, that delicious lemon pasta sounds splendid, and, I suppose a glass of Chardonnay would indeed quench my thirst.

On a Thumbprint

I never thought I'd be the person to have a good leg and a bad leg, and I'm still not. I am someone with a bad thumb, though. By default, that makes my other thumb "good." Before, I just had thumbs. Neutral thumbs. Not good, nor bad, just thumbs. That all changed when I was two months postpartum and shaved off a couple of centimeters of my left thumb with a peeler. I tried to save the slice of skin but it wasn't thick enough for saving, and I haven't touched a peeler since. Actually, that's not true, I held a peeler that looked nothing like the one I hurt myself with but decided it was too soon to put it into action and set it down with such careful precision one might think a bomb was hidden in the handle.

On Caroline Calloway

An interesting figure. An Internet celebrity turned scandal maker turned memoirist. Famous in her own eyes. After her scandal, which consisted of charging people for influencer events that never came to fruition, and pre-memoir writing, she was brought into the limelight by her ex-best friend who "sold her out for a CUT article." Her words, and in her defense, the truth. The article about the scandal maker went viral over a couple of weeks, and for a while she was the bell of the scandal ball. She inspired think pieces, and those think pieces inspired think pieces, and those think pieces inspired a Reddit forum full of tens of thousands of people who claim to hate her, and yet hang on every word she writes and every breath she takes. As a self-admitted privileged, unhinged white woman, she's managed to offend people from all over the world, and she still won't stop. This confidence, this unabashed lack of shame fascinates me. She's been canceled so many times she's now immune to being canceled. Is being canceled a part of her brand, or is it the impetus?

On the Men

I always wanted to be like the men. Bob Dylan. Sam Shepard. John Steinbeck. Leonard Cohen. Dress like them, talk back like them, create like them. I never looked at a woman and thought: I want her life. I mean no offense. Even the most free women were never as free as Bob Dylan, Sam Shepard, John Steinbeck, or Leonard Cohen. The most free woman could go her whole life without mentioning womanhood, and still, she could never escape her gender. She will always be free for a woman, and I always wanted to be like the men. Bob Dylan. Sam Shepard. John Steinbeck. Leonard Cohen. Write like them, talk back like them, create like them.

On Mental Health

When I was suicidal the algorithm kept showing me cheap coffins for sale. Yes, that's right, coffins. I suppose even the algorithm had enough of my empty threats, and after exhausting all the advertisements for online therapeutic services, the next best solution was death. If the algorithm can't turn my depression into an ongoing profit, a one-time purchase will have to do.

The only part I take real umbrage with is how ugly the coffins were. Come to think of it, they were so ugly, I worry the person who created such designs may be suicidal as well. The size of the coffin is another issue altogether. Movement of any kind seems so restrictive that even dead, I think I'd have a panic attack.

On Hollywood—Part 1

Hollywood is dirty and crowded and smells like stale cigarettes. It is not the clean Hollywood Boulevard you see in the movies. The Hollywood Boulevard you see in the movies is fake news. Think of any depiction of Los Angeles like North Korean propaganda. In truth, and in both places, there are an astronomical amount of people starving and dying in unsafe living conditions, but gosh-darn do we know how to make a prop sparkle.

On Hollywood—Part II

I'm walking out of the Five Dollar Store where I work, and someone squeezes my butt with both hands as if each cheek was a stress ball. I turn around and accuse everyone in sight, but for some great mystery, no one confesses. I fast-forward through the potential scenarios that could play out: 1) The guy confesses, and I forgive him because I'm so pleasantly surprised he has the courage to confess. Maybe he even has a condition of sorts that make me feel sorry for him, and offer him another squeeze. 2) Someone else rats him out, a group of strangers, now knights in shining armor pin him to the ground. I call the cops, they take three hours to show up only for the perp to get a scolding, and I am once again, left unsatisfied by the justice system. 3) Someone punches him, and then they get into a fight and—oh no—someone DIES! Now I'm a part of a murder scene. 4) We work out an agreement where I get to squeeze his butt back. 5) Everyone just thinks I'm crazy. We all know the answer, so I let it go, and hold on to it forever at the same time.

ON HOLLYWOOD—PART III

I was walking down Hollywood Boulevard when a tall, shirtless man stopped me. "Ma'am, if your purse is in your backpack, you need to bring it to the front."

"Oh, okay," I said, shifting my backpack to the front of my body as instructed.

"They'll slit your backpack, take your wallet, and run. It's a slit and run." I thanked him for the information. "Tell the other women," he said, and off he went. Not "Tell other women," but "Tell the other women," as if we're all just one being. "I will!" I promised.

On Just Saying Yes

In the theater, we are taught to "Always say yes." It's 2012, I just graduated, and I'm looking for work. My classmate, Cher, an ex-Mormon named after Cher, sends me an email connecting me with a director for a role she was initially supposed to play. The film was supposed to shoot in LA but it moved to the suburbs of Chicago instead. Cher thinks I'd be a perfect fit. It's a "fun little short, and you have the perfect look," she says. "I already sent the director your headshot, and he agrees." I glance at the email only long enough to see my character's name, Lucile B, and write back. "What an honor it is to portray Lucile Ball, especially because of her humanitarian tendencies and incredible talent." The director replies immediately. "Grace, I think you're mistaken," At this period in my life, a lot of sentences start like that, so I remain unfazed. The email continues: "Please see the following character description. Let me know if you're still interested."

I am busy reading a new play and much too desperate, so I do not read the description in full at all. Still, I respond with glee. "This is better than Lucille Ball. Definitely right up my alley!" Ten minutes later, I read the character description and realize I made a terrible mistake.

The character description is as follows:

[Lucile B. Female, 20-30 hot and French, Caucasian, sexy. Need a real "artist" for this character. Lucile B. and her costar, a "director," work together to rattle, shake, and shock their audience with Theology, Religion, Pain, Sex, and Masochism. THERE WILL BE CLOSEUP REPEATED TAKES OF NON-EROTIC NON-NEGOTIABLE SPANK-INGS. For Lucile B, it is easier to be a hysterical tramp begging to be punished, a nasty sex slave eager for pain, than it is for her to mourn her cold dead soul.

While this character and I do have things in common at this point, like nudity, hysteria, and fear. I wish I had come up with something better than "Definitely right up my alley!" The director has attached links to his other short films to "take a look at his style."

All his "short films" open in some eerie desert somewhere off Highway 66. There's hardly any dialogue, but there is a lot of violent sexual intercourse. They all end with the leading lady bludgeoned, beaten, or killed. No matter what, the women always come to their fateful demise stripped naked on a truck. I forward the links to Cher and my friend Andrew. I need a second opinion about how I've agreed to perish in a snuff film. They decide I need to join witness protection immediately. I'm about to write back to the director and decline the role when a slew of texts roll in. I should have known. The director put a tracker on the links and was notified the second I sent them to other people.

To my surprise, he understands how disturbing his footage is and why I'd want to get a second opinion. Turns out, he has a complex artistic vision. He's actually an intersectional feminist, and he will send me all his research. "Trust me," he says, "These films have a purpose in the creative space."

Just Kidding. The slew of text messages I receive in the next few hours range from the tantrums of a little boy who didn't get his way to criminally insane. I know better than to call the cops. Putting my name next to his on some official document would be much worse than enduring his rant. Before I block him, he includes me in a text he sends to Cher: "FUCK YOU" he says, "For recommending someone so unprofessional!"

Cher calls me immediately. I don't even say hello, "He's a psycho," she says.

"And you agreed to be in this movie!?"

"Really!? "Honestly...." She said with her Orange County accent in full bloom, "I didn't read the character bio either..."

On First Impressions

When I gave a speech at my Dad's 60th and made a joke about being the "difficult child," this woman I'd never met, three sheets to the wind, screamed "I've heard about you!"

ON BECKETT

My dog Beckett is a perfect specimen. He is my dream dog. The kind of dog I imagined having as a kid, but never got, because our landlords didn't like happiness. I don't know if it's slow manifestation or kismet, but he's finally in my life.

For Beckett, it's all about vibes. I tried to find a pattern to no avail. For awhile my husband said he didn't like old people, and it made me feel like trash, how could I raise an ageist? How did he become radicalized right in front of me? But thank goodness it's not true. Further research proved he happened not to like a certain group of elderly people, but he doesn't judge me for anything, ever, and I will not judge him. In fact, in solidarity, I do not like this certain group of elderly people either. Actually, on second thought, I hate them.

ON TEETH

An untreated tooth infection will ruin you. I had an infected molar in 2011 and was keeled over for a week straight before emergency surgery. Not only did I have to miss rehearsals for the play I was in, but one of the professors tried to steal my part while I was under anesthesia. The play was Equus, I was the magistrate, and after all that suffering, I was a force to be reckoned with.

ON THE AMERICAN DREAM

The sickest I ever got was a combination of E. coli and a virus. One second I was dancing in my living room, and the next, I was in the bathroom, exhuming everything I'd ever consumed since the beginning of my existence. I was naked and afraid for a week straight. I should've gone to the hospital, but I didn't have insurance, and I couldn't afford a six-figure bill, so like my compatriots, I just waited it out and hoped I wouldn't die.

On Advice

One day while I was sipping on coffee before rehearsal, minding my own business, and scrolling through the fake news on my phone, a woman walked by me with her cute kid. Her kid waved to me, and I waved back. The mom took this is as an opening to converse, "Don't worry, honey. You can be an older mom too." I thanked her, because my appropriate responses are limited. Then she closed her eyes and nodded in that way you do when you feel really good about yourself. She was the wise sage offering a piece of wisdom to what she thought was a younger version of herself. She thought she was relieving me of some societal burden, but little did she know I have so many societal burdens that relieving me of just one doesn't make a dent.

Next time someone interrupts my day to deeply intuit something with perfect accuracy, they better do it right. Don't shake up my world for one word of wisdom, make it three. Buy me a coffee, sit and pray with me, offer me a job. I'm not interested in being a supporting character in someone's cinematic moment of the day. Make me a star or make me nothing.

On Getting COVID

Yes, I was wearing a mask, yes, I was vaccinated, and yes, even boosted, and yes, I still got COVID at Costco. I must say though, it feels like an act of patriotism.

Where else was I going to get COVID? Traveling to some awesome island overseas? Please, I was in the trenches. When my grandkids ask how I got COVID, I'll say, "My story is my neighbor's story. We were just stocking up for the end of the world in the country's, nay, the world's largest retailer of prime and choice beef."

On Long Term Effects of COVID

People are angrier than I remember. Which says a lot, because I ran into some pretty furious people prior to 2020. This bout of rage is different though, it is incessant, and the triggers appear infinite. Were people always this angry about people cutting them off in traffic and accidentally pulling in their driveway, or did people who already felt wronged by the world just stock up on guns during the pandemic?

Sometimes I still lose my taste when I'm stressed out, and my heart beats faster easier. When I got COVID I missed my smell the most, so now each morning, I pause under a certain tree of pink flowers. The intricate notes of the Bougainvillea shoot dopamine straight to my heart and for a moment I forget the world is on fire.

ON BEING A RECLUSE

For the past six months, prior to this trip, I've only left the house to walk my dog and go to my friend's house for Shabbat. I'm a recluse, but with some exceptions. A recluse light. A diet recluse.

I used to hike, I used to go to the coffee shop, I used to go to the grocery store, I used to go the movies, I used to go to the theater, to comedy shows, and one day, I hit my limit. Why do anything, when I could just—not? Everything became an Olympic event, and I did not have Olympian energy or Olympic training.

The fact that I made it to the Netherlands this past March is a miracle. I don't know what forced me. I'd like to say sheer will, but I lost that a long time ago too. Perhaps it was just one tiny little light flickering in my heart begging for a charge.

On Hannah

When I worked at the bookstore in my early twenties, I often worked with a Jewish woman about ten years my senior. She was biding time before becoming a social worker, and I enjoyed our shifts together. She had a similar sense of humor and having grown up in Marin herself, she taught me not to get ruffled by the posh Mill Valley crowd. The only time I ever saw her unfurl was on Wednesdays when an elderly German couple came in. And they came every Wednesday like clockwork. The first Wednesday we worked together, Hannah warned me that they would be coming. "Their accents trigger me," she said. "I hate ringing them up. I hate looking at them, and I hate hearing them speak." Hannah wasn't one to make a fuss about a lot, so I accepted her hatred as intergenerational trauma rearing its ugly head, and felt no need to sway her opinion and say, "Aw come on, Hannah, give them a chance." I didn't need to do a deep dive into her personal history to realize why she was so bothered by their presence, so I agreed to ring them up myself while she'd take her break with a chamomile tea. They weren't warm people, but they weren't raising their right arm and saluting Hitler either, at least not in the bookstore. I hadn't been around a lot of elderly Germans, or any Germans actually, but for some reason, after these bookstore Germans, a portal opened, and I started to run into more. My brother in law's mother-in-law was an elderly German lady who married an Oklahoma military man who guarded some of the most dangerous Nazis during his time in the service. A year before she passed, she told me she remembered how some of her friends "went missing." I was honored she spoke to me about such a time. Then when I was in graduate school, the professor I connected to most was a German woman in her fifties with a thick German accent. Even though she was far from elderly, she wasn't too far from Germany's history, and I thought of Hannah, and how she might be triggered. The irony is Frieda understood me in a way no other professor did. Her straight-forward nature and brilliance made me excited to learn. I saw some of my male classmates try to bully and test her like they always did with women professors, and she wiped the floor clean with them, with ease, with humor and wit and more intelligence in her pinky than they could muster in their entire lives. I admired her, and the tumultuous history of our people was actually an unspoken bond. A master of structure, she taught me how to write better, and she was honest when my work sucked, and when she said my work was good, I trusted her. She became my go-to and someone I'd recommend to other artists needing guidance, and when I think of Frieda, I think my friend Hannah from the bookstore might even like her.

On Disappointment

Jewish elders worry that education about the Holocaust is dwindling. They worry that with so few Holocaust survivors left in the world, there'll be no one to tell the stories firsthand and the truth will be filtered through a system in which our history is forever lost.

As a Jew who grew up in Catholic schools, I was surprised to hear this, because throughout my education, the Holocaust was never left out of our history lessons. Then I started seeing videos, and online conversations that made me think the elders were on to something. Then I went to Anne Frank's house in Amsterdam, and now I'm positive the elders are onto something.

I don't know what I expected. I've seen the videos of tourists at Auschwitz, acting like they're at Disney World instead of the historical landmark of a genocide.

So why was I so surprised when I saw people posing in front of Anne Frank's house like they were at the Hollywood sign? A line of people waiting to snap a selfie smiling ear to ear, peace signs galore, pointing to her name with glee.

For a moment I thought that maybe I should be grateful people care at all, and then I thought, no, I'm a Jew, and it's tradition to be disgruntled, and it's actually my birthright to be disturbed.

On Delusion

I miss being delusional. Now that my frontal lobe is fully developed and I've gone to therapy, I have self-awareness and coping skills and live in the nightmare of reality, and I hate people who are delusional. But I only hate them because I'm jealous. I wish I could return to the version of myself that didn't care. Sure, she was blunted by a pharmacy of anti-depressants, but she avoided hard feelings the way a bat avoids light. I enjoyed the dark, and now I'm exposed. I am especially jealous of the writers who think they are God's gift to the universe. I laugh that they will go their whole lives without ever writing a beautiful sentence, but if they have the self-confidence to think every sentence they write is beautiful, perhaps the joke is on me.

ON AMERICAN TRAUMA

Wherever I go, I think I might be shot dead. There's at least a possibility. The bagel place, the used bookstore, my OB's office, any and all grocery stores, parking lots, walking down the street, the movies, driving in the car, riding in the car, getting in and out of the car. I had a nightmare the other night that I got shot at a university for being Jewish, so that was a double trauma playing out for the price of one.

Americans have a reputation for saying whatever's on their mind, for being uncouth, and oversharers, but I don't hear us talk much about this. Instead of asking each other how we are, we should ask, "Where did you think about getting shot today?" "What did you think when you dropped off your kids at school this morning?" "How many exits did you look for when you went to the mall?"

I followed some of the parents on Twitter after Uvalde. My therapist advised against this, but I felt like it was cruel to leave these parents screaming into a void. I wanted to be a witness to their grief, because it was all I could do. I was traumatized from the tragedy, and I felt guilty, because I knew my grief couldn't even imagine their grief. My grief didn't pale in comparison. No, comparatively, my grief didn't even exist.

ON THE BUTTERFLIES, THE CROW, MY DOG, A SQUIRREL AND THE VIEW FROM MY WINDOW

I live across the street from a man-made butterfly garden. The night my grandmother passed she came to me in a dream and told me to look for her in the butterflies. I have every day since. For nine years. And now after almost a decade, they just appear. I made friends with a crow. It started off slow. He sat on the telephone wires outside my window and stared into my soul day after day. Finally, I offered him one singular goldfish and he took it, and then half a piece of cheese, and then some challah to make sure he wasn't antisemitic. My dog, Beckett doesn't like the crow, but he absolutely hates this one particular squirrel. I know it's the same squirrel because he has a certain attitude about him. He's almost as clever as Beckett who has learned to unbuckle his seatbelt in recent days. The squirrel tries to go for the food left out for the crows, but the crow is bigger and overpowers him. I tried to maintain a magical relationship with the crows but they started pooping all over our steps. I guess my snacks were not up to par. I hesitate to speak ill of the crow though, lest he already knows how to read.

On LA in 2009

When I first discovered Los Angeles, I was in my early twenties going to school in Orange County and working as an extra on film sets during the summer. At that point in time, Los Angeles seemed so huge. In 2009 there were no influencers, just movie stars, musicians, and wannabes. Samuel French, the theatre and film bookshop still existed, and I'd spend hours sitting in the back reading new plays, people watching, and imagining what my future career would look like. I even sat next to a certain disgraced filmmaker at one of my professor's plays, and to no one's surprise, he had no semblance of personal space. Every time he thought something was funny, he'd elbow me in jest. Hard. Coming from the theater, I didn't understand I was supposed to worship someone like him, or even introduce myself for that matter, so I spent that night rather annoyed.

ON THE WORST AUDITION

"I'm just going to do this one at a time," Peter, the director said. "Come on in, let's get started." The moment I walked into the room, I knew I should have left. The room was completely dark, except a little lamp on the ground with a fake candle in the center. There was also some classical music playing, which would have been peaceful under other circumstances, but in this case, felt ominous. "Grace, this is a big part," said the director, "it's a lead, and there are only three people out of everyone I saw at auditions who have the emotional capacity to do it. Tell me. How do you relate to Medea?" How do I relate to a woman who goes "crazy," because all these men are trying to control her, and then goes even "crazier" as she realizes that her husband is a dangerous and disloyal opportunist until she murders her children for revenge/protection depending on your interpretation?

"Um? I feel like she's a really strong woman, and so am I?"

"Yes, perfect, let's just read this side here," he said. We both kneeled down under the lone lamp on the floor so we could see the script. The audition side turned out to be the climax of the play, where Medea has a nervous breakdown. Shockingly to both the director and myself, I was not prepared to have a nervous breakdown, but I now saw the reason for the pitch-black room and the classical music. It was a two-person scene.

"I'm just going to act with you," he said. It kept getting worse. He stopped five lines in. "She's lost her children, Grace, this woman is in pain." So I did it again, screaming louder, because that's what actors do when they are at a loss.

"No, I don't want you to scream, Grace, I want you to really feel." Oh he wants me to cry, I thought. He should have just said so. So I cried, I squeezed those little drops of water from my eyes and let my mascara run forming slides of black doom across my cheek just like he wanted. Again, he tried to sell me the role. "Grace, this is a really good part, and I know you haven't been put on the main stage yet, but this is a lead part, and she has a lot of lines." She has a lot of lines? Well, that's all that matters! Count me in! How many letters do all her lines have? How many spaces between lines? How many characters altogether? Commas? Periods? How many of said lines are fragmented, and how many, end on a vowel? She has a lot of lines? What kind of stupid do they think I am? Actually, when I first started acting in high school, I did used to count my lines to make sure I had the most. But still, this was college. I was not counting lines anymore, at least not out loud.

On Faux Social Media Therapy

While it has its perks, social media is a cesspool of faux expertise, especially when it comes to mental health. Not apologizing for anything or having any empathy for other people has been rebranded to self-care. Feeling guilty about being an asshole? No, don't, that's just someone gaslighting you. It turns out, that everyone is actually perfect, and anyone who has the audacity to question or ask more of you is just trying to guilt you into becoming someone you're not, that person might be a better version of yourself, but it's not your business what anyone else thinks of you, right?

Careful not to have any difficult conversations, or have a disagreement where you provide historical and personal context to your perspective, because you might actually be trauma dumping. And the last thing you want to do is make someone uncomfortable, because being uncomfortable is basically equivalent to dying, and life is just too short not to live, laugh, and love all day every day. Most importantly, just remember to forgive yourself for every mistake you make and hold everyone else's against them forever.

ON WHY

It was important to me to figure out why, when, where, and how I'd come to this. Contrary to how the media often portrays psychotherapists, not all of them are interested in your entire background or what led you to become the person you are today. In fact, some schools of thought believe that the "reason" for things is not as important as how it affects your life today, and are more focused on how to make positive changes moving forward. This works for a lot of people. It does not work for me. I am obsessive. Meticulous. An Excavator.

I needed to know how it happened. I needed to collect the mixed-up puzzle pieces, and then I needed to take those pieces and put them under a microscope. When I put it all together, the discovery that I came to was not necessarily unique, but at least I could see clearly that my "breakthrough" or "year without music" or "awakening," was not caused by one truth coming to surface, but many truths. It was a nuclear reaction of reality that came crashing down around me, and as I put the puzzle together with my therapist I mourned for my old self until I saw the puzzle in a different light one day. I hadn't changed, no, I was just being introduced to my self for the first time.

On the Hypocrisy

I hate how when people willingly leave the earth at my age, other people are like "Oh and they were so young. They had everything in front of them." But when they were alive, they weren't treated like that. When they were alive they felt old, like it was too late, like life had passed them by. "They were so young," implies there's some hope available for their future, but when they were alive, they were skewered. We treat the dead better than the living. Especially the ones who leave too early.

On Humility

I was under the impression that humility comes naturally after a fall. That it's a guarantee that if someone does something so out of step with humanity, humility will eventually follow. I am prepared to see people fall from grace. That's human. What I wasn't prepared for was to watch someone make mistake after mistake, and spew lie after lie, only to end up at rock bottom and not change at all. To show zero remorse, and zero humility. The brazen arrogance is almost admirable, the ability to "stick with your shit," as my favorite improv teacher says, is a gift.

At first, the jealousy kept me up at night. How could someone be so insufferable and still love themselves so much? How could someone be at the lowest point in their lives and have the audacity to look down on others? How could someone mess up this bad and stay so entitled? It wasn't even drugs, it just came naturally, and for that I envied them.

Perhaps the great awakening I was hoping for only happens in the movie version of life. Maybe I've been to too many AA & NA meetings with my friends where people have to practice self-awareness to stay alive. I even considered that I might be looking at a sociopath, but I think a proper sociopath would know that they had to at least pretend to feel bad.

On Specificity

I will not talk about the thing that happened. It makes me too seen. Too vulnerable. Like when you're listening to music on your headphones in public, but then your headphones disconnect, and everyone can all of a sudden hear the melodramatic song you were listening to. If I talk or write about the thing that happened to people who have a different idea about the thing that happened then I won't be able to talk about other things. Everything will be about this thing and I cannot have my whole existence be about this thing. Though there might come a time when it is, because history has shown that there was a time when it was. But if I can avoid the thing, I will, because in person, almost everyone avoids the thing. It's only online where they talk about the thing, or maybe they just don't talk about the thing to me, which is wild since I'm someone who probably knows about the thing better than the people they're talking to about it. Do they think about the thing when they're with me? I don't want to think about that. If I talk about the thing that happened, then I have to fight about it, and I do not want to fight anymore because there is no fighting, there is only condemning, there is only assuming, there is only vitriol and misinformation, and then I wonder if I don't talk about the thing, does that mean the thing will happen again? Is that what happened? Did too many of us stop talking about the other thing that came before this thing?

On the Heatwave or the Beginning of the End

Years ago a heatwave in Los Angeles nearly killed me. There was no escaping it. Even when I escaped into the freezing AC I did not find relief. The blasting AC only served as a reminder that there was a heatwave outside. There was no relaxing, either. The sole purpose of the AC was to cool myself down enough to go back out in the heat.

It wasn't just the heat though, it was the thick humidity slow-cooking me alive from the inside out. I spent all week Googling, "Can heatwaves cause nervous breakdowns?" And I wasn't alone. There were forums upon forums. And sure, the question seems stupid at face value, because it's like asking if lighting yourself on fire will burn, but I was just one of many wondering why I could no longer function as a somewhat normal human being.

During this particular heatwave I went back to my days in Chicago and recalled that whenever it got hot in Chicago, crime rose significantly, but I just figured that's because more people were outside, therefore there was more crime, not necessarily because people were losing their fucking minds.

On Paradise

Perfect isn't good enough, sorry. The beach, the sun, the clear skies, and year-round-every-day's-the-same weather. This it's always summer paradise is oppressing. Grieving in a heatwave is a special kind of torture. Impossible to survive both. Seasons are here to create a sense of reason. Give someone something to work with. Even the youngest of the three, Irina, knew that grief needs to walk, grief needs to work, grief needs wind, and rain, and snow, grief needs something to rail against.

But they'll call you crazy. Who wouldn't want this? Make it a story, put it on your feed, make it a reel, a TikTok, a caption where they say: "Everybody wants this." They'll scream, tell you you're unappreciative of the perfect stolen paradise. And you say okay, okay, okay, enough, and the heat makes you slow, which makes you rot, and you die inside, but everyone is finally happy with you when you're finally someone you're not.

ON THE MOST BRILLIANT OPERA SINGER

I know the most brilliant opera singer. But you don't. She is riddled with grief. This is a different person than the most Brilliant Actress riddled with alcoholism. The most brilliant opera singer experienced grief early on in life and never quite got over it. What came first, I wonder: The grief or the gift? When I went to the Van Gogh exhibit with my husband in Amsterdam, they made a point to mention that Van Gogh's gift had nothing to do with his suffering. They made sure to tell us that he didn't create because of his condition but in spite of it. I thought it was the right message, the responsible message. I don't have the answer, and I'm not particularly interested in it, but I agree with the museum that you don't want someone cutting their ear off on your watch in hopes they'll be the next Van Gogh. What a mess.

ON SELF HELP

People often tell people suffering from addiction and depression or both, "You have to want to help yourself." I always found it rather condescending, and a bit dick-ish. What do you mean I have to want to help myself? What if I don't want to! HELLO! That's the problem! That's the emergency!

Perhaps what's meant by that statement is, that when help is offered, you have to want to accept it. It's your choice. If people could reach that part of our soul they would. I've met those kind of helpers, the ones who are empathetic to a fault, who hurt themselves trying to save others.

The part of your soul that makes you that sick is only accessible to you. Whether you believe in God or not is irrelevant, it's still a fight between you and something bigger than the moment in front of you. That fight is a dark valley, and no one can get you out of the valley, it's almost impossible. There's no map detailed enough, because every dark valley is different. What remains the same is that fear and isolation and darkness. So you have to find your own escape route, and when helpers come to offer torches, your eyes have to be open, and you have to spit out the dirt you've been choking on, reach out, and take the torches. It's surprising what a few beams of light can do.

ON POCKETS

I have always felt out of place in my home state, not like a tourist but an alien. Like my skin and emotional makeup weren't made for this climate. It's too hot in Southern California, but the north is haunted, and Central California, despite its significant agricultural contributions, does not quite fit me right either. But there are pockets of home. Like the Mill Valley Library, where I read myself back to life after my grandma passed, and the smell of the Redwoods surrounding the building helped me breathe again. Like the 5AM walk to the Depot Bookstore where I'd run into deer who looked just as surprised to see me as I was to see them. Or in North Beach, eating fresh focaccia from the Soroccoa Bakery, sitting on the stools at Golden Boy's Pizza, or the alley between Vesuvio's and City Lights Bookstore. Or in the backyard of the Williams' house, where Jack Hirshman asked my mom to look over his work. And as of late, I suppose I've found a pocket at the Whole Foods in Sherman Oaks.

As a creature of habit, I am comforted being surrounded by other creatures of habit. I do not talk to them, but they see me, and I see them. The old Slavic woman who's always blowing her nose with a variety of soups in front of her as she watches a show on her iPad. The seventy-something-year-old Jewish gentleman with black cowboy boots who smokes weed outside with two beautiful lushes, the guy taking bets who always leaves his bag of crab shells behind for someone else to pick up, or the Indian lady who does an energy cleansing ritual every time we make eye contact, the teacher who hates children who comes for her evening glass of wine and fills out applications for other jobs, the happiest bartender I've ever met who won't let anyone break his spirit and says things like, "It's all about how you finish," with zero irony, and then the traditional bartender who is sick of everyone's shit but is actually the glue of the entire community. I love them all. Maybe there is a home here. But as a Californian, I never feel at home at the beach. Never the beach. I actually don't like the beach very much. Too much sand.

On Postpartum Depression

After what my OB referred to as a "traumatic birth,"
I expected to suffer from some baby blues. Like most
things that have happened in the past few years, I had
a nice little plan, and that nice little plan was thrown
out the window and replaced with a horror show.
So, I counted on postpartum depression the way
one counts on receiving an Amazon Prime package.
It would come, and no matter how much damage it
inflicted upon humankind or the environment, it
would come as fast as possible. Imagine my surprise
when it never came. I thanked the universe for know-
ing I had already suffered enough and played with the
idea that there was nothing to deliver since I already
owned depression in every brand, size, and color.

I read that postpartum depression comes with an
identity crisis. An identity crisis? Child's play. To
have an identity crisis, one would need to have a firm
grip on their identity to begin with. The identity of
"Mom" is so concrete and irremovable that I understand how it could feel suffocating to some, but becoming a mother has forced me into the present. The
time I usually devote to self-loathing is now realloca-
ted to making sure I keep a living, breathing, innocent
baby alive and happy. It could be a lot worse, and it
has been. I used to pray I wouldn't wake up in the
morning, and now I care about things like sugar in-
take and the effects of microplastics. I make appoint-
ments for regular teeth cleanings. There are moments
when I don't even recognize myself anymore, but

maybe that's a good thing for someone like me. Then, there are the moments when I recognize myself all too well.

On Washing Your Hands

It was during COVID when I realized how disgusting everyone was. Mostly, myself. I washed my hands for six seconds in the women's restroom at an airport and finished before the woman who had arrived before me. She looked at me like I'd just smeared poop across my face. Complete and total disgust. That's when I started singing the ABCs in my head every time I washed my hands. I didn't want to be the recipient of that look again for as long as I lived, which might not have been long if I didn't re-evaluate my sanitary habits. Like many, my hands became dried up and cracked at the peak of the pandemic. Dawn dish soap and hand sanitizer were used all day, every day.

Becoming a mother to a baby was the second time I realized how disgusting everyone was. I had learned my lesson, but it seemed other people had not. They wanted to pretend COVID never happened, a bad dream, instead of a potentially fatal warning. As a new mom I've become the hand-washing police. Have you washed your hands? Will you wash your hands? Did you see if they washed their hands? My sister, who is also a new mom, is also a part of the hand washing police force. I didn't see them wash their hands. Can you believe they never wash their hands!?

They only washed their hands for three seconds, barely let the water run. We are not the kind of people to berate people into doing what we want, but motherhood makes you who you need to be.

The only people who have given me grief are people over the age of fifty and one young sociopathic Pilates instructor. It is not a ridiculous request. If I didn't have a child, I'd say, hey, smear poop all over your face, for all I care. Eat it. Bathe in it. You'd think I was asking people to douse their entire bodies in disinfectant. Or that I'm implying that they're dirty, but I'm not implying anything, I'm straight up telling you that your hands are full of dirty germs that I have no intention of spreading to my child for the sake of your fragile feelings. If that rubs you the wrong way, you don't need to hold my baby. It's a win-win. You're not doing me any favors by holding my child. I'm not sick of holding my child. I'm sick of cleaning. You love germs that much, be like a three-year-old at Sea World and lick the ground. Just don't kiss my baby afterward.

On the Fair

At the San Diego fair I was able to eat a deep-fried Snickers for the first time in my life. Second to getting COVID at Costco, it was the most patriotic thing I've ever done. I haven't been to many fairs, besides the Renaissance Festival as a little girl, so I didn't realize that the whole point of the fair is the fair food. And then you go and throw it all up on the rides. Unfortunately, I couldn't participate in the latter half because pregnant people aren't allowed to have fun, so I just watched other people throw up instead, which was actually a nice change of pace. I also saw two cows. One was sleeping, and the other one, Gerri, was being used as a model for the dairy presentation. My husband and I sat down on bales of hay and listened to a sweet farmhand make dairy puns about Gerri and her job on the ranch. Then a shinier man with shiny clothes and no calluses on his hands took over to give us a history lesson, and when he said his great-great Dutch grandfather came over from the Netherlands right after WWII and bought a bunch of land and started their family legacy I checked out. How nice for them. It wasn't a complete waste though, the young women next to me were in deep conversation about future prospects, and I learned that there are three types of hot: Dirtbag Hot, Gas Station Hot, and Farmer Hot.

ON RAPPORT

My therapist told me out of all her clients, she has the best rapport with me. That's therapist talk for I'm her favorite. Even though I've grown out of needing to be the favorite, it still feels good. When we met, I was so afraid, ashamed, broken and now she uses me as an example (while still maintaining my anonymity) of what happens when therapeutic tools are properly utilized. An example of mental health? Me!? Now I've heard it all.

ON MOMMY MESSAGE BOARDS

The mommy message boards are less a place where we give each other advice and more a dumpster fire of stories about men who keep the bar lowered into pits of hell. Here are some examples:

I don't know if I'm overreacting, but I haven't slept in 17 days, and I make 6 different meals for each of my husband's personalities. He works part-time and likes to play video games when he gets home. When I asked him for help last night, he threw the couch off the balcony and threatened a divorce. I'm starting to think this isn't normal.

Or

My mother-in-law comes over every day to hold my newborn while I make dinner for her, my father-in-law, and my husband. Last night, when I asked them to help with the dishes, they got offended and said that in their day, they would never dream of making their in-laws lift a fork. Also, they kidnapped my newborn for six hours last Tuesday and got him baptized without my permission. When I told my husband we needed to set some boundaries, he punched a hole through the wall and cried himself to sleep. Am I the problem?

Or

I love my baby so much, and I know I was born to be a mother, but it's my sixtieth night in a row doing all the night changes, and since my husband is a germa-phobe, we agreed that he wouldn't have to change a diaper unless he felt comfortable. I thought the love he'd have for his child would change his mind, but now he's jealous and shitting everywhere, so on top of cleaning up after the baby, I have to wipe his ass every three hours too. When I told my mom, she said I should be grateful that I even have a husband who wants to be involved at all because she had nobody except her parents, her aunt, the neighbors, and everyone from church. Am I losing my mind?

Or

I'm literally giving birth right now, and my husband won't let me get an epidural. He said it's bad for the baby, and if he can run the New York marathon, then I can give birth without being "drugged up." I tried talking to his mom, who insisted on being in the room with me, and she said that her son just wants what's best for the baby and that I can't blame him for being responsible. The nurse said it's up to me, but what she doesn't know is that before we got here, my husband made me sign a sixty-page contract that basically says if I don't obey him, me and the baby will live in the basement and only get to go outside when there's an eclipse. Should I be concerned?

Or

A few months after I gave birth, my husband told me he'll never be able to look at me the same way, and wanted to open up our relationship. At first I was really hurt because he knew I was suffering from postpartum depression, but after talking to some of my friends, I decided that it was better to just give him what he wanted since he's the main provider. A few weeks ago, I helped a man out at the grocery store who looked lost. He just so happens to be a part of Denmark's royal family, and we've really hit it off. He tells me how beautiful I am, and for the first time in my life I've experienced the big O. My husband said he couldn't help me finish when we had sex because it was my problem. Anyway, I told my husband about this since we agreed to tell each other about our extra marital affairs, and he's since set the entire kitchen on fire. Me and the baby are huddled up in the bathroom, should we leave?

ON THE WEEK AFTER BIRTH

A week after I give birth, I sit with a nurse, she takes my hands, and we cry together. All she did was look me in the eye and ask how I was doing. Even though I'm all stitched up, I still feel like my guts are on display, and her kindness turns me into a weeping willow. "We don't talk about it. Nobody talks about it," she says. "Our bodies go through so much, and we put this pressure on ourselves to be perfect. We're supposed to teach our babies sign language, for god's sake." Now we laugh together. "It's okay if they don't learn sign language," she says, handing me a tissue. "When I gave birth, it felt like my body wasn't even mine anymore. It was so invasive, I think it's why I only had one." When the OB comes in and examines the fresh, razor-thin scar above my bikini line, she does a chef's kiss to the air. "The surgeons did an incredible job," she says. If she's pleased, I trust her. I still haven't looked.

On the Nurse from Ukraine— Part I

The day I get induced, one of my nurses is a woman from Ukraine. She sees my last name and says, "Oh, Evanoff. Are you Ukrainian?" I don't feel like explaining that Evanoff is my married name, that my husband is Assyrian, and that they escaped the Ottomans to Russia and-and-and-and-and. Besides, I can see the look in her eyes. I know it well. That desperate need to connect.

And why over-explain when I can just tell the truth? "My great-grandmother was from Odesa," I tell her. "But we're Jewish." I say, "But we're Jewish," because the whole reason my great-grandparents had to leave Eastern Europe was because we weren't considered European. She peers into my soul for a moment, and I can feel her thinking. "You're Ukrainian," she decides.

"Alright," I say like she's telling me the price of fancy cheese at the farmer's market that I'll pretend to mull over before saying, "I'll be back." She can tell I'm unsure, so she insists. "Like me," she says, "Ukrainian." What is this part of the spirit that inspires one to search for a moment of kinship where there wasn't one before? While bombs drop in her home country, she tries to build a bridge in another. I will not forget her.

On the Nurse from Ukraine— Part II

The Nurse from Ukraine stays with me almost all day. At some point, I can't handle the contractions anymore and opt for an epidural. "I had an epidural at two centimeters," she says,

"Why suffer more?" While a doctor puts a needle in my back, she cradles my head in her hands with a kind of tenderness one might cradle an injured bird and says, "It's really important that you stay still. Just look at me." As the needle enters my spine, she says, "You're doing so good. You're so strong. We're almost done. You're about to feel so much better."

Under sedation, I learn more about her life. She still has family in Ukraine, surviving the war. One story that sticks with me is about her sister. When the war started, she escaped to the States, but she didn't know anyone except her sister, and she didn't have any community, and she couldn't walk anywhere, so she decided to go back. The nurse from Ukraine told me she said,

"I'd rather be there with people, even with the war." I guess her sister understands that loneliness can be fatal too.

On Closure

It's the second time I've had to end things with a therapist. I never valued the process of closure prior to this experience. Before therapy, closure felt abrupt and oftentimes too painful to face, so I never did it properly. Instead, I used the block button like I was playing slots in Vegas, so sure that this one move could solve all my problems. In my defense, it did solve some of them. I am still a big advocate of the block button and encourage people to use it with abandon if that's what the moment calls for. I didn't want to end things with this therapist, but the company she works for is tired of working with my insurance company, and I think I might need a break from professional processing once a week anyway.

I knew I liked her when I would lie about my Internet not working. My Internet always works. But I didn't want her to feel bad that her Internet was cutting out, so I always blamed the server on my end. The server on my end worked perfectly, though. Lightning fast. Zero lag. And when we said our goodbyes today and her Internet cut out and disrupted our overpriced session, I told her it was my Internet's fault. I even went one step further. "My Internet really sucks," I said, "It's the worst Internet in the whole country. I'm so sorry."

On the Race

You have to write the spell down before you forget. Before it escapes forever, or is given to someone who will put their first draft on the Internet. Like the women before you, you have to get scratched by the weeds, snipped by the clothing wire, and scolded for running by water as you race to a pen.

You have to stop what you're doing now to do this. You have to be free but imprisoned, abandoned but taken, disciplined but uninhibited. It's impossible one second and only unstoppable for an instant. Ask yourself for permission but never forgiveness.

Write it down, hurry. It's not yours, it's a visitor, and once you see it, it's already leaving.

ON BREASTFEEDING

Rest in peace to all my nice blouses. Rest in peace to all my nice pants. Rest in peace to all my dresses. And God Bless the sleep. That never stood a chance.

I leak from the right boob. I leak from the left. I'm beholden to these cow-like udders. Attached to this small human chest. The milk comes too fast. The milk comes too slow. You will never be enough. You need the perfect flow

ON TJ & DAVE

I want to be around people who know who TJ &
Dave are. I want to know people who watched them
in the old IO in Wrigleyville, before they separated
greatness from the masses. I want to be around people
who remember when TJ could look out at the audience and actually make out peoples faces, before the
stage got bigger and the spotlights got brighter. Not
to say they weren't meant for big stages and bright
spotlights, or to say that they were a stranger to them
—they weren't. By the time I discovered TJ & Dave
they were already legends with a sort of celebrity sta-
tus, but once a week they'd perform in the old IO in
Wrigleyville with old black rickety chairs and even
older black rickety tables. It cost ten dollars and barely sat forty people. They wore no costumes, no stage
makeup, there was no fancy lighting, and they had
no script. "Trust us," they'd say, "This is all made up."
On one particular below-freezing Chicago night,
without any costumes, without any fancy lighting,
or planned music, Dave played an older woman with
zero irony. The way he lifted the invisible teacup and
laid his hand upon his heart, while looking at his
scene partner, TJ, stayed with me not just because of
the duo's craftsmanship, precision, and commitment,
but because it was so tenderly honest, and vulnerable,
and in that sense—a frightening reminder of how
fragile humans are. I haven't seen better theatre since.

ON "FINDING YOUR VOICE"

Observation is the great revealer of perspective. Acting school taught me this. Really, Stansislavky, Meisner, Lee Strasburg, Chekhov, and Stella Adler taught me this. Observation reveals what you love, what you fear, what you need, what you have, and what you're missing, and that is where you will find this voice you're looking for. What do you notice on your walks? What books have you read lately? What keeps you up at night? Who do you see in a crowd? What music speaks to you? How do you feel when you look at a painting? Do you look at paintings? Or do you prefer to paddle out on your surfboard far enough so you can only hear the crash of ocean waves and breathe in the horizon? Or maybe you find beauty in the dinner you're making tonight. Or maybe you see the ugliness of the world. We need that too. Maybe you find your purpose in a cause, in a fight that needs to be fought. Maybe you ride your bike up mountains to escape your thoughts. Maybe you meditate for hours a day because your capacity for peace is just as large as your capacity for war. Tell us about these moments. Start with a grain of sand, your grain of sand specifically, and build a castle so fragile, so sensitive, it crumbles to the touch. If you can shake off the worry about it being pretty or perfect or right or wrong, maybe you'll find your voice.

ON THE LAW

Be loud, American woman. Scream, laugh with your jaw open so they can count your fillings, and guffaw at all your crass freedom. Be loud, American woman. Then tiptoe across state lines, don't tell them where you're going, lie, steal, cheat, survive. When you're faced with hell, you take up a new religion. Be loud, American woman. Scream, laugh with your jaw open, but stay ever so polite, and ever so quiet, ever so obedient, American Woman, so they don't suspect what's coming. So they can tell you to die, eat your dinner, and count your blessings that you were born here with all your crass freedom, ungrateful, wretched, sinful, unstoppable, evil, you incredulous, incredible, American woman.

Be loud, but stay ready. Dust off your cowboy boots, collect your old change, put your trust in a stranger, go on, and get on your way. Practice begging for mercy at the altar of men with less than half of your vision but twice your strength, learn to slither the route of the snakes because you'll need them to live, convince them you're nothing but a lost little meek, scared "what would I do without you," everything, American woman.

About the Author

Grace Evanoff lives in Sherman Oaks, California, with her husband, her toddler, and her dog who won't stop stealing her toddler's food. When she comes up for air, she writes.